New Moon

Friendship

How to Make, Keep, and Grow Your Friendships

The New Moon Books Girls Editorial Board

Flynn Berry · Lauren Calhoun · Ashley Cofell

Morgan Fykes · Katie Hedberg · Elizabeth Larsson

Priscilla Mendoza · Julia Peters-Axtell · Caitlin Stern

CROWN PUBLISHERS, INC. NEW YORK

For every girl who has been touched by the power of a friend

Published by Crown Publishers, Inc., a Random House company, 201 East 50th Street, New York, New York 10022.

CROWN and colophon are trademarks of Random House, Inc.

www.randomhouse.com/kids

Printed in the United States of America

Library of Congress Cataloging-in-Publication Data
New moon. Friendship / the New moon books girls editorial board. —1st ed.
p.   cm.
Includes bibliographical references.
Summary: Discusses friendships and how they affect our lives. Includes practical advice, activities, and suggestions for meeting people.
ISBN 0-517-88581-6 (trade pbk.) — ISBN 0-517-88582-4 (lib. bdg.)
1. Friendship—Juvenile literature. 2. Girls—Conduct of life—Juvenile literature. [1. Friendship.]
I. New Moon (Duluth, Minn.)
BJ1533.F8N48   1999
158.2'5'08352—dc21   99-24037

10 9 8 7 6 5 4 3 2 1
First Edition

New Moon is a registered trademark of New Moon Publishing, Incorporated.

CONTENTS

The folks who made this book want to thank all the people who gave such enthusiastic help and who believe so strongly in Listening to Girls!

The Girls Editorial Board of *New Moon: The Magazine for Girls and Their Dreams,* the girls who read and create *New Moon* magazine, the New Moon Publishing team, and our parents.

Jennifer Cecil, Sheila Eldred, Seth Godin Productions, Bridget Grosser, Mavis Gruver, Debra Kass Orenstein, Joe Kelly, Nia Kelly, Erin Lyons, Jason Mandell, Deb Mylin, Sarah Silbert, Barbara Stretchberry, and Ann Weinerman.

Our colleagues at Lark Productions: Robin Dellabough, Lisa DiMona, and Karen Watts.

And our friends at Crown Publishing: Simon Boughton, Andrea Cascardi, Nancy Hinkel, and Isabel Warren-Lynch.

New Moon is a magazine that gives girls the power to believe in ourselves, to help us stand up for what we think is right, and, most of all, to let us just be girls. *New Moon* sends a message that makes a girl feel, "However I am, I'm okay." *New Moon* describes girls who take action when things are unfair, instead of keeping quiet. And *New Moon* is a fun, safe place where girls know that they are not alone.

New Moon: The Magazine for Girls and Their Dreams is an international, advertising-free bimonthly that is edited BY girls between ages 8 and 14. The recipient of dozens of awards, *New Moon* was twice named winner of the Parents' Choice Foundation Gold Award—the only child-edited magazine ever to win that honor. Begun in 1993, *New Moon* is a girl-driven alternative to magazines and other media that focus on how girls look. *New Moon*'s slant is that makeup, boys, and fashion are important to girls, but they represent maybe three degrees of a girl's life. *New Moon* focuses on the other 357 degrees of a thinking girl's life. Instead of telling girls who they *should* be, *New Moon* tells the world who girls really *are*.

This series of New Moon Books continues that mission. Our books talk about real issues and real girls. They don't say, "This is how you have to be." Instead, they share girls' experiences, feelings, and ideas. Just like *New Moon* magazine, New Moon Books are created BY girls. We chose nine *New Moon* readers from all over the country, including Alaska and Hawaii, Minnesota and New York, to work on the books. They range in age from 10 to 14 and represent homeschool, public school, and private school. White, Black, Filipino, and Asian, these girls have done a marvelous job, as we knew they would.

In this book, they take a realistic look at one of the most important parts of any girl's existence: friendship. Working with Robin Dellabough of Lark Productions and Joe Kelly of New Moon Publishing, they explore different kinds of friends—younger and older, boys and "best." They fearlessly discuss friendship's challenging moments, offering girl-to-girl advice on triangles, fights, loss, and moral dilemmas. An entire chapter is devoted to suggestions for making new friends, especially for those who might be shy. The girls' favorite section—and ours, too—contains dozens of ways for girls to just have fun with friends.

We think you'll love this book because it's about real girls—because real girls created it. So get ready to Listen to Girls, which is our favorite thing to do!

Molly McKinnon
Editor, *New Moon: The Magazine for Girls and Their Dreams*

Nancy Gruver
Founder & Publisher, New Moon Publishing

⭐ Note from the New Moon Books Girls Editorial Board

We are very proud to be the Girls Editorial Board for these books. We hope that they will help other girls feel good about themselves and their abilities. Like you, we are strong, spirited girls. We got together at a hotel in New York to start creating the books. We had an awesome weekend, where we worked hard and played hard. We came up with ideas for most of the material in the books and had a say in everything that went into them. We chose topics that we wanted to write about, too. After that, we worked on the books and with each other over the Internet. And when each book was almost finished, we edited it and said what should change. All in all, it was a pretty amazing experience!

We appreciate New Moon's approach and feel lucky to be reaching more girls through this series of books. Sure, some of us may like boys and putting on makeup, but we also enjoy playing sports, spending time with our friends, learning about international happenings, reading, writing, and all of the other exciting things the world has to offer. That's why we researched and wrote about friendship, earning money, reading, writing, and sports — things that are important to girls in their lives. We found, in the United States and around the world, girls with competence and self-respect. We hope that you will find, in their experiences, the inspiration that every girl needs. Girls are so much more than clothes and diets; we are individuals with views and ideas, energy and talent. New Moon is our voice. Add yours and let us be heard!

Flynn Berry, age 11, New York
Lauren Calhoun, age 13, Hawaii
Ashley Cofell, age 10, Minnesota
Morgan Fykes, age 12, Washington, D.C.
Katie Hedberg, age 11, Minnesota

Elizabeth Larsson, age 12, New Jersey
Priscilla Mendoza, age 11, California
Julia Peters-Axtell, age 14, Minnesota
Caitlin Stern, age 13, Alaska

CHAPTER ONE

What Makes a Friend a Friend?

A friend can tell you things you do not even want to tell yourself.

—Frances Ward Weller

What do you look for in a friend? Someone to pass notes with, to go on bike rides with, someone to keep you company when you're sick? Everyone likes their friends for different reasons, but generally we are all looking for the same qualities. We want a friend to laugh with and cry with, play with and work with, talk with and listen to. Most everyone would agree that being a friend means being honest, being patient, being dependable, and, most important, being yourself.

The True You Is the Best You

Are you a strong person? Do you have a strong self-image? Being yourself is one of the best things you can do. And your friends are probably some of the best things in your life. They can be good influences and role models. But you should not have to copy them. Remember: You are yourself, not someone else. Copying a friend takes away from your own image and puts someone else's image in your place. Your friends like you for who *you* are! Nobody is interested in becoming friends with fake or phony people. Do the things that make you happy and let your natural self shine.

Not acting like yourself and changing your attitude and thoughts for a friend will show; your new friend will probably like you more with your real personality. Stay true to your soul. Your soul is your essence — who you really are — so nourish it and do not try to change or hurt it in any way.

Girl Talk

No one takes the word "friend" seriously enough—so many people throw it around as if it doesn't mean anything. Girls say to me, "You're not my friend anymore." They will not talk to me—only about me—and they make me miserable. But people like that aren't capable of being true friends. I have finally found my personality, because I found true friends this year. It takes courage to be a true friend, and most people do not have that strength.

You and Your Friends' Personalities

Sometimes friends get frustrated because they think your personality changes around different friends and they don't think you are acting like yourself. You *are* acting like yourself, but you may be reacting to your friends' energy levels or senses of humor. Different friends bring out different sides of your personality. If one friend who's quiet doesn't like it when you get silly with your friend who loves to laugh, you could explain that her personality is not the same as your other friend's and that you enjoy hanging out with her as much as with your other friend.

A Friendly Checklist

Rank the qualities you look for in a friend in order of importance to you. Now check yourself against your list. How do you rate? How do your friends rate?

Animal lover	Honest	Sincere
Athletic	Independent	Smart
Book lover	Kind	Strong
Brave	Neat (as in tidy)	Wild
Creative	Organized	Willing to dream
Curious	Patient	Willing to take
Energetic	Perfectionist	the blame
Generous	Practical	Willing to try
Good listener	Punctual	new things
Graceful	Sense of humor	
Hardworking	Shy	

Quiz Yourselves

Think you know everything about your friend? Think again! Take this quiz and see how much you and your friend really know about each other. Answer all the questions from your friend's point of view, while she takes it for herself. Then reverse roles: She fills out the quiz the way she thinks you would answer, and you fill it out for yourself. When you're done, compare answers to see how much you actually know about each other. It's okay if you do not answer all of the questions correctly. It just means you have more time ahead to get to know your friend even better.

1. Who is your favorite author?
2. When is your birthday?
3. What does your mother do?
4. What's your favorite kind of animal?
5. What do you like to do more than anything with your friends?
6. What's your best subject in school?
7. If you were a flower, which one would you be?
8. What religion are you?
9. Do you speak another language besides English?
10. Would you rather go to a baseball game or a musical?
11. If you could live in any other period of time, which one would you choose?
12. What is your favorite vacation spot?

13. What is your strongest personality asset?
14. What would you like to change about yourself?
15. Who are you closest to among all your relatives?

Different Kinds of Friendship

There are many different kinds of friends. Friends may be of a different race or of a different sex. Their personalities can be completely opposite, or they can be as alike as identical twins. No matter what the differences are, friends should respect each other for who they are and not for what they want the other to be. Friendship should create a balance between differences. Lots of girls have friends who are older or younger than they are, or boy friends, or a friend who's a cousin, stepsister, or some other relation. Friendships are unique, each posing new challenges and offering special times.

Friends are what make life fun. I have lots of friends. I have two women friends, who help me through the hard times with their wisdom. I have one friend who's a boy. I have a good friend who lives in Japan. She stayed a month with us. Cashiro taught me a lot about other countries. And then I have my girlfriends.

Girl Talk

Best Friends

Often, a girl has one best friend, but really she can have a number of best friends. The term "best" usually describes a friend you can trust with anything you tell her, and with whom you can be completely yourself. A best friend is there when you need her. She can lift your spirits. She knows you so well it is scary. Sometimes a best friend is a relief from a world that tends to misunderstand you. With a best friend, you can ask for an opinion and usually hear the truth. When you ask, "Does this look good?" and you hear, "Maybe you should try something else," you don't feel angry or offended. You feel good knowing that there is a person out there willing to help you and guide you honestly. If you were away on vacation and your parents allowed you to make only one long-distance phone call, picking the person to call would be simple.

Some people think that having a best friend is more negative than positive. The words "best friend" exclude people because they elevate one person over others. Saying "close friend" is less exclusive and allows other friends to be close, too. If you mention your best friend when you're with a larger group of friends, others can get jealous and feel hurt or left out.

7

It is all right to have a best friend. Most people — though not all — do have best friends, so don't feel as if you're being mean to other people for picking one special friend to be your best. Try not to give another friend mixed signals that you two are best friends when you're not. Just say, "You know you're one of my good friends." That will get the message across without being mean or hurtful.

POINT OF VIEW: *Best Friends*

It is sometimes very complicated to have best friends. One of my friends and I were getting to be very good friends when I was already best friends with another girl. The girl who I thought was a "good" friend thought she was my "best" friend. She ended up getting hurt and mad at me. I told her that I wasn't trying to give out mixed signals and that she was one of my really good friends.

I remember I was really scared that a girl I thought was my best friend didn't think of me as her best friend. I finally knew she did when I realized that we talked to each other on the phone every day. It always feels special when my best friend says to other people that we're best friends. Pretty soon people feel natural always saying your names in one hello because you and your best friend are always together. That is how it is for me and my best friend—we are known as *SilviaandJulia*, or *JuliaandSilvia*.

—Julia, age 14, Minnesota

Boys as Friends

Having a boy as a friend can be great. He can be just as fun as any of your girlfriends, and he is also a friend whom you can confide in and seek advice from. Whenever you have a problem, he will most likely be there to help by offering insight that a girlfriend may not have, especially when it comes to other boys. Think of him as just another friend with whom you can share many moments of laughter, secrets, and memories.

When my family and I found out that my mom had cancer, my two best friends, Silvia and Andrew, helped me out, listened to my fears, and supported me through everything. Andrew and Silvia go to my church, and they prayed for my mom. They also said, "Oh, your mom is looking better," and, "Don't worry, she won't die." They just kept feeding me encouraging words that got me through.

Girl Talk

POINT OF VIEW: *Boy Friends*

I was eight years old when I met Josh. Our parents decided that if they were friends, their kids should be, too. The next thing I knew, I was sitting next to my brother on someone's couch, staring across the living room at this strange-looking boy. He stared right back. After a few uncomfortable moments, our parents suggested that we go swimming in the creek that ran through the backyard. We grabbed our towels and trekked off through the backyard. The moment we were out of sight, Josh started talking. He hasn't stopped since. We spent the rest of the day having water fights, laughing, and talking. For several years, we went swimming, camping, and sledding together whenever we could.

Suddenly, our parents stopped trusting us when we were together. The first time we noticed it, Josh and I were in his room doing homework. We had shut the door so that we wouldn't be disturbed. Later that night, Josh called me. He told me that after I left, his dad grounded him for having a girl in his room with the door shut. We couldn't figure out why our parents were acting so weird. We concocted many theories to explain their behavior; our favorite was that aliens had kidnapped their brains. It took a lot of explaining and a few arguments before we convinced our parents to put as much faith in our friendship as we did.

* * *

On the first day of seventh grade, I discovered that there were two rules. The first: Girls stayed on one side of the hall, boys stayed on the other. The second: If you dared to cross that invisible line, you only did it to ask someone out. I didn't understand the game, and I didn't want to play it. Boys were much more interesting to talk to than about, but no one else thought so. I didn't have any friends on the girls' side, and I couldn't cross the line to find any on the boys' side.

One day, my brother brought a weird, skinny guy named Erik home with him. We hit it off right away, and we became best friends. I never imagined our friendship would create so many problems for our classmates and teachers.

People tried hard to take our friendship away. They didn't understand that my friends and I are not made up entirely of our sexuality. That is only a part of who we are, a part that has little to do with our interactions and nothing to do with our friendships. Erik and Josh are still two of my closest friends. Had we followed our school's rules, we never would have stayed friends. Looking back on the times we've spent together, I realize how glad I am that I didn't stay on the girls' side of the hall.

—Rain, age 18, North Carolina

Friends of Different Ages

Sometimes a friend may be older or younger than you. You may discover more about yourself by being with someone who can offer a different point of view. A coach, a doctor, a teacher, or even a relative can be a friend. An older friend has been through what lies ahead, and a younger friend challenges you to be a good role model to look up to.

Lifelong companions and best friends Helen Keller and her teacher Anne Sullivan are one of history's best-known examples of friends of different ages. Their unique relationship began on March 3, 1887. Years later, Helen celebrated that day as her "soul's birthday."

When twenty-year-old Anne arrived at Helen's home in Alabama, she found a rambunctious six-year-old girl waiting for her. Helen had lost her sight and hearing when she was nineteen months old, and her parents hadn't disciplined her since then. Spoiled and used to doing whatever she pleased, Helen was totally unprepared for her teacher's strict rules and manners. One day at breakfast, Helen tried to grab some food from Anne's plate. When Anne refused to let Helen have her way, Helen threw a tantrum, kicking and screaming. She tried grabbing some more food. Refused a second time, Helen pinched Anne and received a slap in return.

Soon, however, Anne began teaching more pleasant lessons to the child who rarely smiled and hadn't laughed since she became deaf and blind. One day, Anne ran to Helen, laughing merrily. She placed Helen's hand on her smiling face and traced the word "laugh" on her hand with her fingers. Then she started tickling Helen until she was laughing, too. Soon Helen was quite a different child, "splashing radiant joy," according to the book Helen wrote about Anne.

As Helen's teacher, Anne's most celebrated accomplishment was getting Helen to understand the concept of language. Beginning almost the minute she arrived, Anne spelled words into Helen's hand, starting with "D-O-L-L" for the doll she gave Helen as a welcoming gift. Helen quickly caught on that if she spelled "C-A-K-E" into Anne's hands, she would get to eat a slice. Only a month after Anne arrived, Helen made her famous discovery at the well: As Helen held her hand under the spout, Anne spelled "W-A-T-E-R" into the other hand, and as the water started gushing, Helen suddenly understood the connection.

I have a lot of friends, but my very best friend is my grandma. I love her so much, and she is really nice. We do a lot of things together. I feel like I can talk to her about anything in the whole world and she would listen and understand. Our friendship is one of the most important things to me, and I could never, ever have another friend as sweet and understanding as my grandma.

Girl Talk

CHAPTER TWO

Great Good Friends

Hold a true friend with both of your hands.
                              —African proverb

Overcoming Challenges in Friendship

Even though friends are one of the most enjoyable aspects of life, nothing is ever perfect. Friendships have their ups and downs. Some negative situations can arise between friends, like fighting or name-calling, but there is usually some remedy you can try that has worked for other girls.

When Your Friends Fight

One of the worst things two friends can do to you is make you choose between them when they don't get along. During their tiff, try not to favor one friend over the other. Try your best to keep your friendship with both. If it looks like they aren't going to become friends again, and you still like both of them, explain that their fight has nothing to do with you and that you still want to be friends with both of them. It may be a tightrope walk, but you will make it.

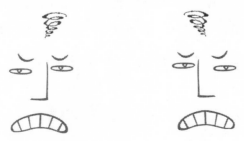

Speaking Your Mind

"I told my best friend something really personal, and she blurted it out in front of everyone. Now I do not feel like I can trust her."

Sound familiar? It may not make you feel any better, but this stuff happens to just about everyone — and more than once. We all get into situations where there are problems in our friendships we're scared to face. But giving in to that fear and keeping silent isn't the best solution: If you are feeling bad because your friend seems to be ignoring you and you say nothing, you could very well lose that friendship. It takes some courage to communicate your thoughts and feelings.

Take the case of the longtime friends in the quotation above. When her friend revealed her secret in front of everyone, the girl who had the secret was really embarrassed, but even more hurt that her friend would take her confidence so lightly. Still, she was scared that if she brought it up, it would start a fight and she'd lose the friend forever. Finally, though, she realized that their friendship just wasn't the same with this problem in the way; she didn't feel like they could talk anymore, and she felt lonely. So one day, she said what was on her mind — how hurt she was, how she missed her best friend. Turns out, the girl who blabbed had been feeling really guilty about what she'd done, but had been scared to confront her friend about it. They talked and talked, and soon enough they were talking and giggling like nothing ever happened.

Of course, not every situation is solved this way. Putting yourself out there and saying what you think and feel is risky — there is the possibility that you will embarrass yourself, and you may not get what you want. But on the other hand, you may get exactly what you want! Either way, you'll know that you gave it your best shot.

Ask a Girl

"My friend is always having serious family problems and coming to me for help because she doesn't have anyone else to talk to. I'm not sure how to help."

Having a friend burdened with family problems can sometimes burden you, but your friend sounds like she really needs you, so here are a few tips.

1. Your friend probably needs to get away from her home. Invite her for a weekend to your house. Get together with a group of friends and do stuff.

19

2. LISTEN TO HER!!! When she calls you up or talks to you, she probably just needs to have a listener. Give her suggestions about what to do, and ask questions. Talking about her problem will make her feel better. If she doesn't want to talk about it, let her know that you are always ready to listen.

3. Let her spill her emotions. If she wants to cry, let her. Try to comfort and console her.

4. If you do not know what to do, tell a grownup. It can make you feel better. Make sure that she/he knows the girl. A parent is often helpful and can give suggestions.

5. DO NOT TELL ANY OF YOUR FRIENDS. Telling a grownup is okay, but telling another friend will not help. She doesn't need to have her problems spread across school.

6. Don't try to take charge of your friend's problems, but welcome her to talk and confide in you. I hope that you can help your friend; she needs you. ◈

Saying It

A good way to express your reactions to someone else's behavior is to use *I-messages*. That way, you're letting your friend know how you feel and why you feel the way you do, without accusing or attacking her. Criticizing your friend or telling her what she is doing wrong will usually make her defensive. But describing how her behavior makes you feel will increase your chances of being heard.

"I kind of like this guy, and I think that he likes me, too, but when I talk to him, my friends act all mad and ignore me."

Let's look at the situation described above — you like a guy, but your friends become cold to you whenever you start talking to him. One response is *You guys make me feel really bad when you ignore me just because I'm talking to John.* The problem here is that you're telling your friends how they are *making* you feel, and are immediately putting them on the defensive. Instead, tell them how you *do* feel, by saying something like *I feel bad when you guys seem upset because I'm talking to John. I like him, but I don't want things to change between us… I still want to be friends with you. I really want us all to do something together so you can get to know him. I think you'd probably like him, too.*

Here's the basic formula for I-messages:

I feel _____ (your feeling)

when you _____ (describe their behavior),

because _____ (the impact on you).

I would like_____ (what you want).

Keep in mind that you can do everything right and still not get what you want. You have control only over what *you* say, not over how people will receive your message or how they'll respond. Your friends might appreciate your honesty and be relieved that you still want to be friends with them. Or they may still feel jealous of your new friend and continue to punish you. Being clear about how you feel and what you want is a risk. It feels awkward at first, but if you start communicating clearly and honestly, maybe your friends will, too.

Aggressive, Passive, or Just Right?

In any problem situation with friends, there are usually three ways to respond. Let's say you and a group of friends are deciding where to eat lunch. One of them makes a strong case for pizza, and the others agree. You've already had pizza twice this week. What can you do? You can do and say nothing, simply going along with the group. That's a *passive* response. On the other hand, you could be *aggressive*, blurting out, *Oh, no, not pizza! I'll throw up if I have to eat pizza again today. If you go there, I'm eating lunch in the cafeteria.*

Both these ways of behaving hurt you in the end. If you're passive, you wind up resentful (not to mention that you're stuck eating something you don't want!). Okay, so in the pizza situation, keeping quiet may not be a huge disaster. But when it's a big decision, you damage your self-esteem by not sticking up for yourself, and you damage your friendships by being dishonest about how you feel. Meanwhile, if you're aggressive, you annoy your friends and start alienating them, making it nearly impossible for them to *want* to change their minds.

What about taking more of a compromise approach — something like *I'm a little sick of pizza. Would you guys mind if we ate at the diner today and the pizzeria tomorrow? Or how about the deli?* This *assertive* style is a good tactic. You've expressed how you really feel and why you feel that way without sounding bossy or harsh, and you've given your friends some reasonable options. You've shown respect for both your own feelings and the feelings of your friends.

Ask a Girl

"Out of thirty kids, there are fourteen girls in my class. The girls have a very hard time getting along. They separate into two groups: a group of popular girls (five girls) and a group of less popular girls. At recess we sit on either side of the field and glare at each other. My teacher doesn't understand how we feel. One of the girls keeps asking, 'Why can't we all be friends?' I don't think it is possible. Do you?"

In my school, we also have a "popular" group. But they're certainly not very popular with the other groups. I have noticed that popular groups are only popular within their own group. My friends and I do not really like the popular group, but that's okay. We do not hate them, either. Think about it: Why does the unpopular group dislike the popular group, anyway? Just because they're popular?

It may not be possible for all of you to be friends. Some of the girls may not want to be friends. That's okay. Try to put aside the labels and just get to know each other. It's probably a good idea to discuss this with everyone ahead of time. You may have to make the first move. And they may not like it and

get mad at you. Try to keep an open mind. Everyone is enti-
tled to her own opinion, and you do not have to like everyone.

If you succeed in getting to know each other and you still
do not like some people, that's okay. There are plenty of peo-
ple I really can't stand. Everything about them just bugs me.
But I do not go pick a fight. I just leave them alone, and they
leave me alone. I keep my opinions of them to myself or be-
tween myself and friends I trust not to blab.

It's got to be a group effort, and all of you (well, at least
a good number of you) have to try and keep an open mind.
It may be possible to be friends with everyone, but maybe it's
not. You're going to have to try first. I hope you succeed. ◇

Long-Distance Friends

A friend can live anywhere. It doesn't matter who she is or
where she comes from, as long as she is a good friend.

In any long-distance friendship, there are ways to keep
in touch. For a friend who is moving away, you could get
an address book and have all of her friends put their ad-
dresses and phone numbers in it. You could also make a
videotape of all of her friends saying good-bye. You could
make a good-bye packet and put in things like photos,

articles about friends, videos, autograph books, books, pencils, tapes, pens, stationery, journals, stamps, an address book, a phone book with all her friends' numbers circled, and envelopes.

Once a friend has moved, try sending audiotapes or videotapes to each other. Start a story, a journal, or a scrapbook, and send it back and forth for each of you to add to. Every month, mail a photo of a fun experience you've had to your friend. And, of course, rely on technology: e-mail, faxes, and telephones!

POINT OF VIEW: *Faraway Friends*

The summer that I was seven, a family came to stay with some friends of ours. I went to the ferry terminal to meet them and gave their eight-year-old daughter some shooting-star flowers in a pink cupcake wrapper. We spent the summer together and found that we were into a lot of the same things. We made wood and felt flower fairies, dried flowers for potpourri, and played with dolls. We are still close friends.

Last summer, when I was twelve, my Japanese teacher's niece came to visit for a couple of weeks. She was honest, funny, and daring, three qualities I really like in a friend. It was cool to have someone who was more daring than I was for a change; most of my other friends are either less daring or about the same. And she found ways to laugh at everything, even falling on her face. We had a lot of fun together. This summer, she visited again, and we went camping and swam with a wild dolphin. I hope she comes next summer.

Recently, a girl who will be going to summer camp with me this year e-mailed me and asked if I wanted to be e-pals (e-mail pals). She told me she was into drawing, the Middle Ages, Tamora Pierce, and Philip Pullman (among other things). She sounded friendly and interesting. Now we e-mail each other often. I can't wait to meet her, talk to her, and see what she's like.

—Caitlin, age 13, Alaska

Friendship Around the World

Did you know that girlfriends in Ethiopia live together without their parents during the school week? That Japanese girlfriends traditionally give each other little origami gifts as signs of fellowship? And that while French girls say goodbye with kisses on two cheeks, Belgian girls kiss three times? Different cultures have different friendship customs.

Finding New Friends Far Away

It is easy to make friends with people you have never met before: Get a pen pal! There are tons of sources for finding pen pals, and pen pals can develop into very satisfying friends. *New Moon* magazine lists girls from around the world who would like to write to each other. The list includes each girl's special interests so you can hook up with someone who seems compatible with you. There is also an organization devoted to fostering pen pals:

Friends Forever Pen Pals
P.O. Box 20103
Park West Station
New York, NY 10025

POINT OF VIEW: *Jamaica*

I recently went on a trip to Jamaica with a group of other American girls to build a chicken coop for an orphanage in need. The girls we stayed with and interacted with have been through a lot, but they are much more outgoing and friendly and trusting than most girls I know. They also express friendship differently; when they care about someone, they braid or style that person's hair. It is their way of saying, "Hi, I would like to meet you." They would just come up to you and start playing with your hair. It took about one and a half hours, but they braided it over the stretch of a few nights. Our first reaction was, "Okay, what are you doing to me?" but everyone grew to love the attention. Jamaican girls also show friendship through joking—they weren't shy at all. They'd make up silly nicknames for you.

One very obvious difference between American and Jamaican girls is how they deal with fights. They were never catty, never talked about someone behind her back, never gave someone the silent treatment. When they had a problem, they would be very up-front about it (which can have its disadvantages). The girls were all close (although there were a few bullies) and relied on each other completely.

—Flynn, age 11, New York

POINT OF VIEW: *Ethiopia*

I attend Debre Sina High School in Debre Sina, Ethiopia, which is 195 kilometers, or 121 miles, from Addis Ababa, the capital city. I have two best friends, Almaz and Helen.

Our parents live in a small village outside of Debre Sina called Medina. Almaz, Helen, and I live alone in Debre Sina during the school week. We rely on each other from Monday through Friday. On Friday afternoon, we begin the two-hour journey to our parents' village. Then every Sunday morning, we collect our lunchboxes from our mothers and walk back to Debre Sina.

One Sunday, Almaz, Helen, and I said good-bye to our families, as usual, and began our trip to Debre Sina. Suddenly, heavy raindrops came down. None of us had an umbrella. Our lunchboxes, our books for leisure reading, and every part of our bodies soon became wet.

It was difficult to walk due to the mud and flooding. Soon, we came to a long, wide riverbed that must be crossed to get to Debre Sina. However, because of the heavy rain, it was full of water.

"What can we do?" we said to each other.

"I see one big standing stone in the middle of the river. Now listen to me," advised Helen. "If we jump and rest at the tip of the stone, one by one, we can easily cross it."

"No, we can't, Helen," responded Almaz. "It is impossible. We can't jump such a great distance."

I listened to their conversation attentively but said nothing. Suddenly, Helen jumped and came to rest on the stone's tip. But as soon as she landed, her feet slid and she fell into the water.

At this moment, my body shook violently with fear.

"Help! Help!" we loudly shouted.

Fortunately, there was another standing stone that Helen caught with her hands, and she was able to hold on and save herself. Her lunchbox, book, and only pair of shoes, however, were carried away.

Luckily, a farmer heard our shouting. He had a long walking stick, and he was a strong man. He came across the river by using his walking stick, and he pulled Helen out of the water very quickly. Even though she was safe, she started to cry, because she had no lunchbox with *injera* (bread), no books, and no shoes. We advised her to stop crying, and we made a promise to share our *injera*.

If Helen had listened to everything that Almaz had told her, she never would have been in danger. It is important to accept your best friend's advice.

—Yegle, age 17, Ethiopia

Losing Friends

As people grow up, they also grow apart. Friends who have been inseparable for years may one day feel like they do not know each other as well as they thought they did. The games they used to play no longer entertain them, their inside jokes are forgotten, and the energy they used to create together has fizzled. Although friendships are valuable, they can sometimes fade — not always for an obvious reason, like a fight or finding new friends. Sometimes a distance sets in, and a friendship doesn't seem as strong as it once was.

In other cases, friends just have trouble getting along. Frequent fighting and bickering can be stressful and frustrating. Before calling it quits, the best solution may be to take a break from each other. Friends are important. Do not allow some tension to ruin a good thing. Let time bring you back together and let a misunderstanding work itself out. Try talking to your friend. If she refuses to talk to you, then maybe you should take that as a sign to back off and give her some space. She might not have all her thoughts sorted out yet and may not know what to say to you. Do not jump to conclusions about her, but realize that sometimes letting go is the right thing to do. It's no one person's fault when friends grow apart.

POINT OF VIEW: *Losing Friends*

I had a friend who was really nice. We saw each other almost every day and told each other everything. She had other friends, and that was okay with me; I had other friends, too. But soon she stopped answering my calls and didn't want to see me very often. I invited her over a few times, and when she came, she acted like she was "too cool" for me.

At first, I clung to the relationship like it was the end of the world, but my parents told me I should let her out of the relationship without feeling guilty. That seemed to be what she wanted, so I decided to let her make the next move. No reply.

I called her to tell her I was moving, and all of a sudden she wanted to do things: go to the mall, watch movies, and just hang out. Because we had not seen each other in more than a year, this sudden burst of effort to be friends left me feeling betrayed. It was she who deserted me, anyway, wasn't it? I felt like I was her last resort for a friend, and now that I was moving, she was worried about who she could fall back on. It seemed like her new friends liked me, so why had she left me and started to act too cool for me when she met them? I guess that happens to many best friends, and although I do not have a single best friend, I have many who I like and trust.

—Meaghan, age 13, California

When Not to Keep a Secret

Has your friend ever asked you to cover for her while she slipped out to do something? Should you cover for a friend? Is what she's doing dangerous? Will it harm her physically? Emotionally? Or is it just some silly thing like sneaking out wearing makeup she's not allowed to wear?

Your friend told you not to tell, but you're worried about her and want to tell someone. You feel like you would be betraying your friend. That's common. Is she in danger? Is the problem just too complicated for her to handle? If she is in the tiniest bit of danger, you need to tell someone. If you care for her and want her to be safe, then you've got to tell! She might be angry with you, but in the end, she will thank you. And even if she is angry with you, at least you will know that you did the right thing.

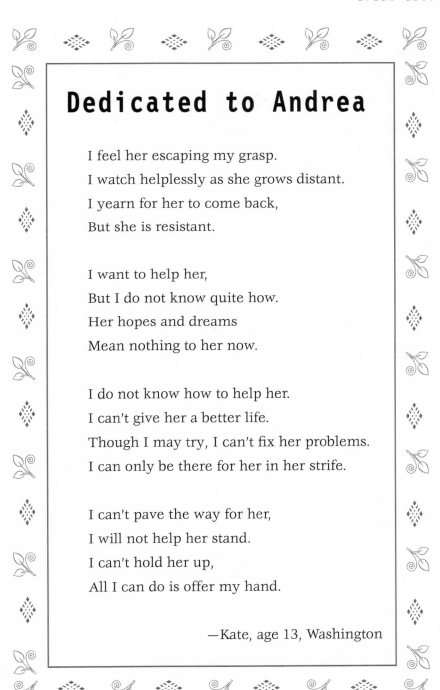

Dedicated to Andrea

I feel her escaping my grasp.
I watch helplessly as she grows distant.
I yearn for her to come back,
But she is resistant.

I want to help her,
But I do not know quite how.
Her hopes and dreams
Mean nothing to her now.

I do not know how to help her.
I can't give her a better life.
Though I may try, I can't fix her problems.
I can only be there for her in her strife.

I can't pave the way for her,
I will not help her stand.
I can't hold her up,
All I can do is offer my hand.

—Kate, age 13, Washington

Standing Up for Your Beliefs

Your beliefs are important, and you need to hold true to them! Just because your friend doesn't believe the same thing doesn't mean either of you needs to change. Respect her beliefs, but also make sure she respects yours. Don't try to make her believe anything she doesn't want to believe.

Sometimes, though, a friend's beliefs differ so vastly from your own that it becomes time to question the friendship. If a friend felt that it was okay to lie or steal under certain circumstances, you might have to break off the relationship.

You need to have your own opinion about things, and you need to know when to say no. But you also need to be open-minded and learn to see all sides of the story. Don't be too judgmental.

Recognize what your friends are feeling. Encourage them to speak out. Do they encourage you, too? A friend should never abuse you verbally or make you feel afraid to speak your mind.

When the Pressure's On

What if someone is pressuring you to do something you don't want to do—something small, like borrowing your CD player or your clothes, or something big, like trying drugs? These strategies can help:

1. Say no and keep repeating it. You don't have to make an excuse like *I'm not feeling well* when you really just don't want to do something. You can give a reason for your answer, but you're not required to.

2. The best defense is a good offense. State how you feel when the other person pressures you. Ask why she or he keeps pressuring you after you have said no.

3. If that still doesn't work, refuse to discuss it further. Walk away or suggest doing something else.

Friends and Religion

Religion can affect friendships in many different ways. Sometimes a friend can believe in a faith so strongly that it colors her outlook on life. If your religion is different from her religion, you may find that your relationship is enriched by the similarities and differences in your outlooks. In fact, your friendship might be strengthened by trying to understand the basic concepts of each other's beliefs.

If you can discuss your perspectives on life, death, and other spiritual questions and appreciate what you can each offer to the friendship, then it can be really interesting. If your friend can't accept who you are and will not let your religious or spiritual views be a part of you, it could become annoying.

Religion is very personal and should be handled with respect between friends. Friends can't always agree, but they can respect each other's beliefs without changing their own.

When my friends and I have different opinions, we try to listen to each other and accept our differences. I have a friend who believes in the Christian religion. I do not. I do not think that either of us is going to be talked out of her opinion. So we do not try to convince each other that ours is the right way. Instead of fighting, we concentrate on other parts of our friendship and talk about other stuff.

Girl Talk

Friendships Within Triangles

Triangles are groups of three friends. Triangles — three-somes — whatever you call them, they're tough. Someone often gets left out. Sometimes two girls are best friends and use the other girl as a last resort. If the best friend can't come over, then one girl invites the third girl over. Often this makes the third girl angry, and when she tells the other two how she feels, they do not see what they're doing. You need to have patience and learn to treat others fairly. And if you're not careful, the tables could turn and one of the best friends could become the third one and the third girl could become one of the "top two." You should make sure that everybody's equal and that there's no top girl in control.

Our advice to girls who are in threesomes is to evaluate your friendships with the others involved. Would you miss the other girls if you never saw them again? Do you enjoy spending time with them? Do you find their friendship truly worthwhile? If it seems worth it, you should stick with it and try to be the best friend you can be to both of them. Threesomes are worth it when you really like both of the other people. If you do not think that your relationship with them is valuable enough, do not get too involved. Back off. Focus on your other friendships; they're what is important.

39

She Started It

All friends bicker or fight from time to time. But fights do not have to be the end of the world — or of your friendship. There are certain rules you can agree on ahead of time with your friends that help make fights fair, if not exactly fun, and ways to react to your friends' anger or bad moods without having an argument.

It is normal to argue now and then. Although you and your friends may have a lot in common, you are still completely different people with different interests and ideas.

If you are angry with a friend, the worst thing you can do is keep it locked up inside. You do not have to yell, scream, or shout to get your point across, but in order to discuss a problem with your friend, you have to approach her nondefensively and with an open mind. Simply explain to her what you are feeling, without attacking her, and ask her if she understands why you are feeling that way. Maybe she will realize that she was wrong or that something needs to be changed. It is always best to communicate.

POINT OF VIEW: *Dealing with Fights*

I think that I fight more with friends I have known for a long time than with new friends. If it makes it any better, a fight could be seen as a sign that you know your friend well enough to feel comfortable expressing your opinions even if they are not the same as your friend's. But I have some friends who I know pretty well and have never had a fight with. Don't feel as though you have to fight with your friends to be really close to them.

I used to fight a lot with one of my closest friends. We would disagree over tiny things, like who got to play with the cutest plastic panda. What worked for us was to get away from each other. We would stomp out, cool off, and the next day go on as if nothing had happened. We never apologized or even talked about the fights after they were over.

Now we don't fight as much as we did before, and it's easier to make up. I know my friend well enough so that when I see that she feels like disagreeing, I try to be extra nice to her until she gets over it. But our old way of dealing with fights used to work really well for us. It doesn't work for everybody, though. In some friendships you need to admit you had a fight, apologize for what you said or did, and forgive your friend. This can be hard, especially if she said something really nasty. But if she really seems to regret it, let it go and move on.

—Caitlin, age 13, Alaska

Forgiving Friends

Forgiveness is a very big part of friendship. Sometimes a friend makes mistakes and hurts you unintentionally or makes you feel unwanted. Then you need to talk with her about what she did to you. That way, she can try to avoid hurting you in the same way again.

Sometimes, though, a friend isn't really a friend and may try to hurt you on purpose. When a friend is intentionally mean to you, you need to talk to her about it and think about finding new friends. After all, is this how you want your friends to treat you? One of the hardest things about losing someone you thought was a good friend is forgiving her in your heart and letting her go. Once she is out of your life (at least partly), you need to let go of your sadness and forgive her for what she did to you. It is not easy. You will find new friends who are better to you. Don't give up on the kindness in people altogether.

POINT OF VIEW: *Letting Go*

Jill and I were absolutely inseparable. We had been friends since kindergarten and had gone through everything: the death of those closest to us, first kisses, and our parents' divorces. I have never had a friend like her. She was the only person I have ever trusted. I had heard that people changed when they got to high school, but I never thought that would happen to me. Little did I know, but my life would be changing forever. Jill met people who were considered the snobs. She wanted to be with them and not me. Instead of talking about our crushes, she wanted to talk about cars, clothes, and parties. It wasn't that I wasn't interested, but I had other priorities, like school and sports. Nothing seemed to matter to Jill except superficial things. It was as if she had lost all of her values. As the years passed, I saw her less and less. We really don't even talk anymore, but I always remember the fun we had together.

—Lindsey, age 16, California

Your Parents and Your Friends

It can be very hard to have a friend your parents don't approve of or don't like. It might not seem like it, but your parents are almost definitely not trying to hinder your social life. Parents are often right about a "bad" friend. Inspect your relationship with your friend. If you're positive your friend is fine, ask your parents why they don't like your pal. If they just don't like her personality, they probably will tell you and maybe open your eyes about her. Have your parents heard a rumor or lie about this person? If so, be sure to explain that it is untrue. If you're comfortable with your friend, then your parents should at least try to respect her and get along with her. Before they say anything about your friend, ask your parents to get to know her. Arrange a time for your friend to stay for dinner so your parents can talk with her and learn more about her.

Ask a Girl

"My mother has cancer in her brain and lungs. She doesn't smoke, drink, or use any other drugs, so the cancer is not her fault. Everyone at school knows, and feels sorry for me. I wouldn't mind that, but yesterday I found out a group of girls who I thought were my friends were just faking it, and they really think I am completely geeky. I feel stupid and gullible. Now I only have one real friend, and I'm afraid I'm losing her, too. What should I do?"

I'm sorry about your mom. Mine is healthy, so I can only imagine the emotions you are going through. But I can relate to the friend problem. About two months ago, I broke up with my best friends. I still feel terrible about it. Now I only have one close friend, too, but here are some suggestions for you. Start hanging out with a friend who is not so close. You might build another close relationship. Try to hang out with some of your friend's friends. That way, you might make some new friends. IMPORTANT: Ignore your old friends. Do not try to get back at them. It only makes things worse. All the best. ◇

When a Friend Talks Behind Your Back

Sometimes it sneaks up on you and hits you like a bad flu virus…only it hurts much worse. You would rather have had the flu than these nasty creatures in your life. Everyone has had them or will have them, so do not worry, you are not alone. What are we talking about? Finding out that someone you thought was a friend has been talking behind your back. Friends who aren't really friends are actually a blessing (well, maybe not a *blessing!*) in disguise. They help your soul grow, and you become more sensitive to other people's feelings than if you hadn't gone through the experience. (We are only human; we slip up.)

You need to be ready for this situation. When a friend talks behind your back or says nasty things about you, DO NOT HOLD IN YOUR FEELINGS. Get it out of your system in any way you can: by writing in journals, talking to an adult (or a better friend), taking a nice long sprint, or reading a book. If you think it will help or if you are bold enough, you can try to talk to the "friend" straight on and tell her how you feel. You might ask this "friend" why she was so mean to you. Try not to use revenge to let your anger out, because that doesn't fix anything. You will end up in an even worse position, and you will feel like a bad person.

Just let your heart be true to what you think is right.
Never lose your love of life because of one sour apple out
of a whole orchard of shiny, loving ones. You are special—
do not let anyone make you think differently.

Two of my friends and I were hanging out at my house.
"I love you," Sarah told me.
"Sarah and Caitlin sitting in a tree," Meaghan started
chanting.
"Not that kind of love," Sarah said. "I would cry if she died."

That's what makes a friend a friend.

CHAPTER THREE

How to Make New Friends

*Friendship with oneself is all important,
because without it one cannot be friends
with anyone else in the world.*

—Eleanor Roosevelt

There's nothing more exciting than finding a friend who understands you, who you can talk to and have fun with, and there are always going to be times in your life when you want to make new friends. If you move to a new place or start a new school, you definitely need to find friends. But even in your everyday life, as you change and grow, it's normal to want to make new friends who might reflect the new you. That's why it's important to be open to meeting new people.

We don't mean it's easy. But it's not impossible, either. When meeting new people, here's what works for us: Smile. Say hi. Ask some questions. Tell something about yourself. You can't expect other people to make the first move. Show that you're willing to try to make friends. A little bit of friendliness goes a long way.

There are tons of ways to meet new people. There's no reason that you should have the same old friends every single day forever. By participating in an activity that interests you, you can meet people who share your interests. Priscilla, age eleven, from California, came up with a list of the following ways to make new friends:

- Join or start a club.
- Play a part in the school play or an instrument in the band.

- Join a scout troop.

- Take a recreational class outside of school.

- Join a dog-walking circle.

- Take a dive at the neighborhood swimming pool.

- Volunteer.

- Play a team sport.

- Go to camp.

- Find a pen pal.

- Throw a party and ask each guest to bring someone you don't know.

- Log on and find a cyberpal while chatting.

- Become friendly with classmates you haven't talked to before.

- Start a small business, such as a baby-sitting service, with other girls in your neighborhood.

- Ask a classmate to study with you.

- Crack a joke to break the ice.

- Offer someone a small token of friendship.

- Arrange to bike, walk, rollerblade, etc., to school with a classmate.

- Get involved with your religious community.

Through all of these activities, you are bound to meet people. Say you are out walking your dog in your neighborhood or at the park, and see another girl your age. If she looks nice, and approachable, try saying something about an obvious, general topic: *Looks like it's going to rain* or *What a well-behaved dog you have!* If that doesn't get her to respond, you might ask questions, such as *What kind of dog is that?* or *Do you go to school around here?* Once you've exchanged a few words, you can introduce yourself. If she is in your neighborhood, she probably lives close to you, so you can ask her for her phone number or plan on meeting her at the park the next day.

Before introducing yourself to a person or a group, however, you ought to evaluate them. This is not a sign of being judgmental or paranoid; you want to make sure that you make the right friends. If the group is doing something dangerous or unhealthy, like vandalizing or smoking, you probably just want to keep your distance. If they are playing sports or studying at the library, they might be a better crowd for you.

Ask a Girl

"How can I make new friends?"

You might want to take up a class or a sport. That way, you'd be exposed to lots of new people who share your interest. Also, try to initiate a conversation with someone who you don't know very well at least once a day. ◇

Listen Up

When making new friends, of course, you want to make sure to listen to the other person. But there's more to listening than not talking while someone else is speaking, especially when it's a new friend. Listening is a skill, and when you have it down, there are few things that make a friend feel more understood or cared for. And the more you listen to other people, the more you'll be heard. Here are some ways you can be a better listener:

◆ Offer a story of an experience you've had that is like the one she's telling you about, to show her you understand. If your friend is sharing a funny or happy moment,

FRIENDSHIP

It's like an apple.

I look for someone

who will give me half of their apple

or help me pick one of my own,

locking their fingers so I can step into them

and have my feet supported.

Someone who will cradle me

if I fall,

or listen to why I like the green ones

better than the red ones,

and someone who will understand

why I feel that way,

and someone who will make eating an apple

the time of my life.

—Sarah, age 13, Alaska

laughing with her, touching her arm lightly, or murmuring an encouraging *hmm* might be all you need to do.

◆ Ask a follow-up question about what she's said. She'll know you were engaged enough to want to know more. Some people need encouragement to open up.

◆ Keep eye contact with the speaker. That way, she'll know you're paying attention, and you can listen to her expressions as well as her words.

◆ Listen with your body as well as your mind. Body language sends powerful messages. Turning away from your friend while she's talking to you — even if it's just to look at the boy with green hair walking by — might make her feel like you're not really interested in what she has to say.

◆ If you feel like you're not really understanding your friend, tell her what you think you heard so she can correct or confirm your interpretation.

Finding Friends when You Are Shy

Say a new girl just moved to your town. She avoids everyone and sits alone. Would you assume that she was a snob and thought she was too good for everyone else? Well, that could be — but it could also mean that she's shy. Shyness is not unfriendliness or unkindness. Meeting new people can be a scary and intimidating experience sometimes, and being shy only makes those feelings worse.

Why are some people shy? Shyness is usually linked with sensitivity. Put them together, and you have one tough life. Something that can really help is viewing sensitivity as a strength. You realize things that other people wouldn't give a second glance to. You look beyond someone's surface almost naturally. If you're the one who is shy, is it really worth hiding from yourself and other people? Being shy is hard, but it doesn't have to keep you from making friends or having fun. Shyness just means you'll have to push yourself to do things, like talking to someone or doing something independently, that other people find easy.

Try to overcome your shyness one small step at a time. If you're too shy to go up to a person and introduce yourself, write a note. Say, "Would you like to go to the library with me?" Call up a classmate and ask for her help with an assignment, or offer your help to someone who is struggling. Even if you can do it alone, you don't always have to. Other people love to feel needed. One thing to remember is that shyness is often mistaken for rudeness or being unfriendly. Since you may not want to just come out and say that you're not being rude, try giving people a warm smile, say hi, introduce yourself.

Our advice to those who want to get to know shy people is to smile at them, talk to them, ask them questions, tell them about yourself. They may seem intimidated, but inside they are probably welcoming your conversation. Make sure that you look beyond someone's outside, which may seem unfriendly, and give them time to open up and warm up to you. Try to understand them.

Another concern with making friends with someone who is shy or not as popular as others is that you might worry about what your other friends will think. Maybe you see a girl who seems lonely and you'd really like to reach out to her. Our advice is to just do it! Ask her to join you at your regular lunch table in the cafeteria or to walk home with you and a few other girls. You don't need to force the lone girl on your other friends; go slowly and gently so they won't be resentful. If anyone asks you why you're hanging out with so-and-so, try saying what Katie, age twelve, from Minnesota, says: "Because she's nice to me!" After all, that's the bottom line for being a friend. Maybe once your other friends notice that you're really getting satisfaction out of your new relationship, they'll be more convinced to give the formerly lonely girl a try.

Ask a Girl

❝I'm usually a pretty friendly person, but when I meet new people, I'm kind of shy. If I'm with a friend, I'm okay, but by myself, I feel like I don't know what to say. Or maybe I'm afraid people will get annoyed if I say what I'm thinking. What should I do?❞

You should smile, make eye contact (normally when people are nervous, they look down), and say hi. Introduce yourself. Make small talk. If you're, say, in English class, mention how you like the book you're studying in class and ask if they do, too. Let the conversation go from there. Most of all, be true to yourself. ◇

Keep the Old

You love all your friends. You have been close for as long as you can remember. But at some point, you may need a breath of fresh air. It is not that you do not like them anymore, it's just that you need a little variation. You're sick of eating at the same lunch table, laughing at the same jokes...so you start hanging out with that girl from English

57

class. Wow, you think. This girl is really neat. But as you spend more time with her, you notice a weakened relationship between you and your older friends.

Depending on how your old group is feeling, a number of problems could arise. Perhaps they think you ditched them. If this is what they think, whether you did or not, and their friendship still means something to you, the best thing to do is to make sure you still spend time with them, doing the same things you used to do, to keep the friendship alive and strong. Sometimes friends may get jealous and be mean in a situation like this. It is a natural emotion to feel threatened by the presence of another girl stealing away your friend, but again, you both have to work on your friendship, so you should try your best to talk things out. Understand that it's okay to make new friends, but that it is just as important to maintain a connection with the old group. Who knows? Maybe you can all be friends.

Sometimes a short story can capture a mood or feeling like nothing else can. Here's a story that we think describes the source of friendship.

Friendship Central

Once, there was a friendly, fun-loving twelve-year-old girl named Annie, who had just moved to a new country and had to go to a new school. It isn't important to say which country and which school, because this happens in all communities all over the world. Annie had no friends in the school. Nobody even acknowledged her outside of class. She didn't really understand why. She figured that to her classmates, she was a nobody — just one person who didn't count in the endless sea of faces in her large school. But why, she wondered, did she seem to be the only one with no friends?

59

Little did Annie know, she would find the answer soon enough. That night, she had a dream…a dream that would change her life.

Annie felt herself pushed through a door into a large room that resembled a regular office. A secretary sat at a huge desk with papers overflowing and three telephones ringing off the hook.

"Hello, Friendship Central, may I help you?" she said to a caller. "He dumped her? Okay, please dial five for the boyfriend department and then dial sixteen for the breakup department. Okay, thank you, 'bye!"

Annie looked around and saw a corridor that seemed about a mile long. It had many doors, with numbers on them, written in gold. Workers walked in and out; like the secretary, they all wore large smiles. At that moment, the secretary looked up at Annie, grinned, and said, "Hello!"

"Hi," replied Annie.

"Your name?"

"Annie."

"One moment, please." The secretary consulted her larger-than-life computer. "Oh, yes, you're the dreamer. Case 008: new kid with no friends. But don't worry, dear. It will soon change; just a malfunction in one of our computers. Follow your assistant, Bob, to door 173."

"Really, miss, I do not know what's going on. Where am I? How did I get here? Who is Bob?"

"Bob, at your service," said a smiling man who appeared. He was a comical figure in a gray sweatshirt and pink plaid pants. His mass of blond hair resembled the end of a mop. Annie almost laughed out loud but instead considered his feelings and smiled politely.

"A pleasure to meet you, Annie," Bob said as he guided her down the corridor. "For the rest of your stay at Friendship Central, I will be your assistant. I know everything that goes on around here, so I can answer any questions."

"I have a few," said Annie, smiling—since she would now get some answers. "First of all, what is this place, Friendship Central?"

"Friendship Central, or FC, as we locals—"

"How do you become a local?" Annie asked, interrupting Bob in midsentence.

"Oh, that. Well, if you're a particularly great person— you know, friendly and all that stuff—you get imported up here to work at FC. You stay for a while, and when your duties are done, you go back to earth into the soul of the person you left behind."

"Whose soul did you leave behind?"

"I'll let you figure that one out for yourself. Anyway,"

Bob continued with his first answer, "Friendship Central—or FC, as we locals call it—is the headquarters of friendship in the world. We control it all here: good friends, bad friends, girlfriends, boyfriends, 'just friends.'"

"But how?" Annie asked, fascinated by what Bob was telling her.

"Well, that's something called 2C2E (too complicated to explain). But I'll give you the basics. That computer on the secretary's desk? Well, in there are the names of everybody in the world."

"How do they get everyone's name in there? I mean, people are born and die every second!"

"Oh, that's 2C2E. Anyway, that computer connects to a lot of other computers in FC, and all the other computers have all kinds of relationships entered in them. According to our calculations, everyone in the world is supposed to have a friend. But our computers often make mistakes, and people get left without one. That's what happened to you."

"Okay, I think I'm starting to understand. But that still doesn't answer how I got here," Annie said. Meanwhile, a little voice inside her kept saying that she knew this guy Bob.

"You were transported here because tonight, when you went to sleep, you thought about it a lot. If you think about it hard enough, your thoughts are transported into our computers, and *bam!* You come here, and we clear up your little problem. It's my specialty."

"So what you're saying is that my not having any friends is a computer error, and now we're going to get me some friends?" Annie didn't know whether to be happy, because it wasn't her fault she had no friends, or sad, because she always thought friendship happened naturally when two people liked each other.

"Right-o, Annie. I knew when I first saw you that you were a smart kid."

By now, they had walked a long way down the corridor and reached door 173. Entering, they saw an enormous room with a huge computer. Bob stepped up and punched a few of its keys, and a printout came out of the back. Bob read it, smiled, and said, "That's it."

"That's it?" Annie said in disbelief. "The problem is cleared up? I'm no longer friendless?"

"Yep, yep, yep. You are free to go home now," Bob replied.

"But I like it here. When can I come back?" Annie asked anxiously. She didn't want to leave the happiness and friendship she'd found here.

"The next time you think really hard about it. You won't

remember FC until you come back, so you won't know where the friends came from. Just appreciate them the best you can. Good-bye."

And with that, the two shook hands and started walking back down the corridor. Suddenly, Annie realized who Bob was. The soul Bob left behind when he came to FC was Robert's — the best friend Annie left when she moved to her new country.

Instead of telling Bob what she knew, Annie just smiled, because she was pretty sure he knew she would figure it out. She turned and asked her final question: "Where in the universe is this place?"

As the darkness of her bedroom closed around her, Annie saw him gesture to his chest. She understood at once — friendship comes from the heart.

—Erica, age 13, Malaysia

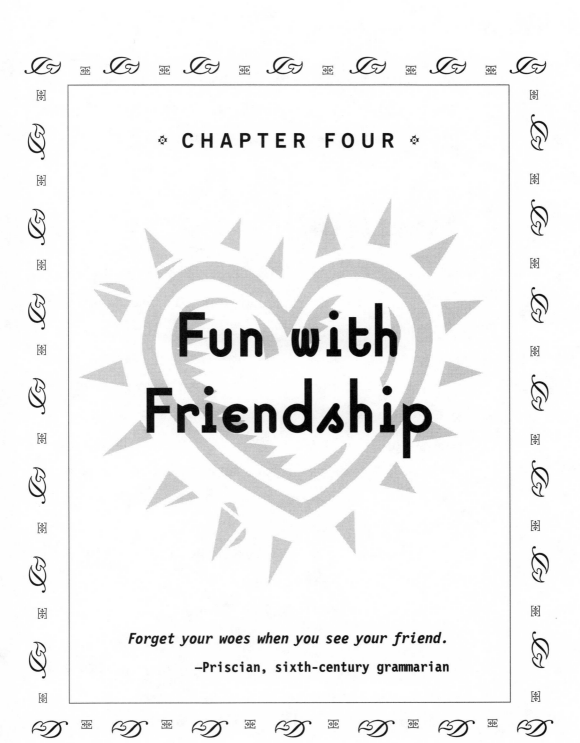

◇ CHAPTER FOUR ◇

Fun with Friendship

Forget your woes when you see your friend.

—Priscian, sixth-century grammarian

We tried to jam this section with neat or nice things that you might not have thought of yet to do with, for, or to your friends. We had fun—hope you do, too!

Tradition!

Whenever you go on a vacation with your family, bring your friend a treat from that area: maple sugar candy from Vermont, saltwater taffy from the beach. It's nice to get a souvenir and know someone was thinking about you.

Make a date with your friend once a week. Meet at a designated time and place and ride bikes to your favorite restaurant. If you go to a pizza place, have a slice of pizza and a milkshake. Make a point of not going there with anyone else. It is something that only the two of you do together. It's your secret.

Be treasure hunters. Every Sunday morning, you could head out, scanning the streets for overlooked riches. Who knows what you might find? A discarded book, a really interesting bottle cap, an old pocket watch. When you've exhausted the neighborhood, carry your discoveries home and add them to your private collection.

Keep a spiral notebook for the two of you to share.

When you write your friend a note or letter, write it in the friendship journal (notebook). When she responds, she will write on the next page. Continue passing it back and forth until you reach the last page. You can read the notebook over when you have time. It is a good way to keep your memories together. Decorate it with stickers and pictures to make it more personal.

Make food a part of your tradition. During lunch on Fridays, you can always have peanut butter and jelly sandwiches, or whatever food it is that both of you love.

During the fall and winter, have a regular Friday night television get-together with a bunch of friends. The weekly event can begin after school, when you load up on edible supplies for the evening. If one of your friends can't make it, the others can call her and "watch" the show together with her over the telephone.

Clubbing It

If you and your friends share a passionate interest, organize a club. For example, let's say you're involved in animal rights. Get your friends together to write bylaws, goals, membership cards, and a schedule of meetings. Maybe your first goal is to raise money: Have a bake sale in your neighborhood and donate the proceeds to the American Society for the Prevention of Cruelty to Animals.

How about a book club? You could call it "Read On" and meet once every two weeks to talk about a book you've all agreed to read. Some months, you could choose books with the same theme; others, you might read all of one author. The local librarian can help you find books and discussion guides to help you get started.

Form a cooking club. Every time you meet, you can exchange recipes and bring your own dish. You can also cook something together. What could be better than being with your friends, eating good food, and taking control of the kitchen for a while? Maybe you could cook dinner for your parents.

Perhaps all of your friends play the same sport, or maybe you all play different sports. Get together after school or on weekends and play different sports together. Rotate teams so that it is always fair.

Form an arts and crafts club. Each week, you could experiment with different media: watercolors and pastels, yarn and beads. Keep a portfolio of all the work you create together. To raise money, you could try to sell some of your creations to family and friends.

It may not sound like fun, but homework can be fun in a group. Sometimes working alone gets boring, and a friend or two can give you the motivation that you need. Have contests like "Who Can Find the Answer First?"

Celebrate Your Friend

Make a card with an acrostic, a poem written so that the first letters of all the lines, when read vertically, spell out your friend's name:

> **J**oy is what you bring to each day.
> **U**nfading is your smile for me.
> **L**ightness seems to be in your step
> **I**n school and on the field.
> **E**xcellence is your middle name.

When you want to let a friend know how much your friendship means to you, write a letter of appreciation. Use a piece of beautiful handmade rag paper and a calligraphy pen, and write out all the things your friend does that make you feel good, that make her a great friend and a great person. Try to be specific, so your friend knows you mean it. Instead of making general comments, single out examples:

General	More Specific
You are so thoughtful.	I'll never forget the time you were late for a party but returned my library books for me anyway.
I like your style.	I love the fact that you wear purple and that you cut your own hair.
You're funny.	You make me laugh when you do your imitation of my mom scolding me.

Do you have a friend who loves some of the songs on the local radio station but complains that the commercials really annoy her? Make a tape recording of her favorite songs, a sort of customized radio station.

Make a sign for your friend's bedroom door: her name spelled out on a piece of wood, brightly painted and covered with sparkles.

Secret Language

Make up your own alphabet so you can communicate in your own language — sort of a secret code. Then, whenever you write each other notes or play games, you can use your alphabet instead of the ABC's. It's fun and gives you a special bond.

Pig Latin

To communicate through pig Latin, you take the first letter of a word and put it at the end of the word, along with an "ay" sound. So if you want to say, "I need to walk my dog," you would say, "I-ay eed-nay oo-tay alk-way I-may og-day."

Double Dutch

When speaking in double Dutch, you first choose the sound that you want to use after the first letter. If the first letter is a vowel, put the sound at the start of the word. You can use "ag," "ob," "ib," or "ig." "I need to walk my dog" would sound like "agI nagEED tagO wagALK magY dagOG."

Sign Language

Sign language is a form of communication used by the deaf and hearing-impaired. It is a good skill to learn, and you and your friends can practice using it with each other.

Symbols of Friendship

Long ago, women gave each other small tokens of friendship. These keepsakes were usually handmade or created from materials found around the house or in nature. A typical nineteenth-century keepsake might have been a feather, a bookmark, a piece of lace, a pin cushion, a needle case, a beautiful stone, or a sachet. A woman would personalize such objects with the initials of both herself and her friend. The main point was that these small gifts were inexpensive and easily tucked into a pillow, a drawer, or a scrapbook.

It is still nice to offer a friend a token of your esteem. There are all sorts of flowers, gemstones, trees, and other objects or symbols that have come to represent friendship over the years. Offering one of these to your friend, or using those symbols in a note, can be a way to say, "I'm really happy we're friends." Here are some friendship symbols:

Amazon stone = Friendship

Blue periwinkle = Early friendship

Carnelian = Friendship in sorrow

Cat's-eye = Platonic love

Cedar = Think of me

Clasped hands = The bonds of friendship

Geranium = True friendship

Ivy = Friendship

Natrolite = Female friendship

Orange blossom = Woman's worth

Snowdrop = Friendship in adversity

Surprise, Surprise!

Invite a friend for breakfast — especially unexpected on a weekday morning. Bake muffins and decorate the dining room by hanging a sheet from the ceiling to create a private breakfast nook.

Once in a while, send an anonymous note to a friend or leave her tiny presents in her locker.

For a birthday surprise, you could get to school early and cover a friend's locker with balloons.

Draw your friends pictures, write them notes, tear out pictures they would like from a magazine—anything. It is really cool to surprise your friends with little gifts that show you were thinking of them.

Call your friend when her favorite song is on the radio and let her listen to it over the phone, or just tell her what station to tune in to.

Party On!

While birthday and holiday parties will always be special, any day can be a fiesta if you have the right attitude. Call up one or two of your friends, turn on the music, and get ready to roll!

Consider holding the following:

- Last Day of School Party
- First Snow Day Party
- Indoor Picnic Party
- Summer Good-bye Party
- Anniversary of the Day We Met Party
- Neighborhood Olympics Party

- Longest Day of the Year Party
- Pet Party
- Rainy Day Party
- Before School Starts Party
- Fashion Show Party
- Picnic Party

A New Moon Sleepover

A sleepover is always a great way to get all of your friends together for a good time. The first step is to make the invitations. Be creative by using colored paper and cutting out a theme shape, like a crescent moon for a New Moon Sleepover. Decorate them with glitter and stickers, write with gold and silver pens, and be sure to include all of the necessary details, like what, where, when, and who.

When everybody arrives, the decorations should add to the theme. Dim the lights or use black lights instead. Decorate the halls with holiday lights and put a strobe light above the dance floor, along with a disco ball. Try turning off all the lights and using only flashlights. Put glow-in-the-dark star stickers on your ceiling and go crazy with streamers and balloons.

Prepare goody bags for all of your guests by including jewelry, friendship bracelets, nail polish, pens, pencils, and stickers. Tell everyone to bring her favorite CDs to rock out to and her favorite movies to watch while eating popcorn. You can also have fun painting each other's nails, doing each other's hair, and dressing up in costumes. Make up cool dance routines to your favorite songs.

Try filming your party on a video camera. Aside from capturing silly moments of fooling around, you can perform plays, dances, or anything else that you can think of. Do a talk show by having your friends choose a host, a couple of people to be the guests, a few to be the studio audience, and others to do the commercial breaks. Then videotape the whole thing and watch it the next morning over breakfast.

Friendship

A glow, a lingering love.

A feeling of sunny days and silver waves,

    gliding over rosy toes

    washed by a gossamer tide,

An effervescent cuddle of affection and love.

A glimmering smile that says

    always and forever,

    your friend I will be.

—Lauren, age 13, Hawaii

Friendship Album

Making a friendship album is one of the best ways to preserve precious memories. You can buy a scrapbook or picture album at the store, or you can make your own. Use sturdy paper and punch two or three holes down the left side, securing the pages with yarn or string. Decorate it and make it pretty to look at by adding sequins, stickers, and paint. In the album put anything that has special meaning to you and your friends or represents a memory that you never want to forget. For example:

- photographs of you and your friends
- pictures of your favorite celebrities
- movie tickets
- letters, notes, or cards
- poems that you have collected or written
- lists of your favorite books and authors
- your handprints traced in ink
- printed-out e-mail messages
- cartoons
- pressed flowers from hikes you've taken
- candy wrappers
- ribbons from gifts you've exchanged

Recite Two-Voice Poems

In a two-voice poem, each person reads one side aloud.
Here's one to get you started:

Friends

Five.	*Five.*
My turn!	
	My toy!
Stop it!	
	I'm telling!
Don't do that!	
	Don't touch that!
I want that!	*I want that!*
	It's mine, anyway!
So?	
Nine.	*Nine.*
Is not!	

Is so!

Bossy!

Stupid!

I hate you!

I'm leaving!   *I'm leaving!*

Teenager.   *Teenager.*

I never said that.

                       I never did that.

You told!

                       You promised!

Jerk!   *Jerk!*

Sorry.   *Sorry.*

—Caitlin, age 13, Alaska

POINT OF VIEW: *Good Times*

I went to the Renaissance Festival with my friend Christina. It was a very, very hot day. We played a game that she was much better at than I was. We both stood under pails of water. First she paid them extra (in secret) to drop an extra pail of water on me. So I got wet right away. The pails were held up by poles. Then we were supposed to throw beanbags at a target that pushed the pole and dumped the pail of water. I was playing with the pole while Christina was getting ready to throw her beanbag at me. All of a sudden, the bucket of water fell down on me because I was playing with the pole that held it up. Then it was my turn because I had gotten dumped on. But I was terrible at it. First I threw two, then they gave me a couple more. Finally, they let me walk closer and closer, and I still kept missing. I was finally so close that the game operator leaned over and whispered in my ear, "It isn't a rule that you have to throw it. When you get close enough, you can just push it." So I pressed the lever, and Christina got soaked even more than I did. It was so hot, we were both happy we got wet.

—Ashley, age 10, Minnesota

CHAPTER FIVE

Finding Out More About Friendship

The comfort of having a friend may be taken away, but not that of having had one.

—Seneca, Roman philosopher

Here's a comprehensive list of resources for the New Moon girl who'd like to keep exploring friendship and having fun with friends.

Books (fiction)

Although nineteenth-century "bosom friends" Anne (of Green Gables) and Diana may not seem to have much in common with modern-day Saskia White and Jane Singh (*The Saskiad*), all of the friends in these books strive for the trust, faith, and loyalty that make friendships last.

Anne of Green Gables (series) by L. M. Montgomery (Puffin Books, 1996)

Annie on My Mind by Nancy Garden (Sunburst; Farrar, Straus & Giroux, 1982)

Bad Girls by Cynthia Voigt (Scholastic, 1996)

The *Betsy-Tacy* books (series) by Maud Hart Lovelace (HarperCollins Children's Books, 1994)

Black Beauty by Anna Sewell (Random House Books for Young Readers, 1986)

The Borrowers by Mary Norton (Harcourt Brace Children's Books, 1998)

Bridge to Terabithia by Katherine Paterson (HarperCollins Children's Books, 1996)

Buffalo Brenda by Jill Pinkwater (Aladdin Paperbacks, 1992)

Charlotte's Web by E. B. White (HarperCollins Children's Books, 1990)

Dangerous Skies by Suzanne Fisher Staples (Farrar, Straus & Giroux, 1996)

Finding Out More About Friendship

Echoes of the White Giraffe by Sook Nyul Choi (Houghton Mifflin, 1993)

The Egypt Game by Zilpha Keatley Snyder (Bantam Doubleday Dell, 1996)

Flight of the Albatross by Deborah Savage (Houghton Mifflin, 1989)

The Friends by Rosa Guy (Henry Holt & Co., 1973)

The Friendship by Mildred D. Taylor (Bantam Doubleday Dell, 1987)

A Girl Named Sooner by Suzanne Clauser (Avon Books, 1976)

Harriet the Spy by Louise Fitzhugh (HarperCollins Children's Books, 1996)

Huckleberry Finn by Mark Twain (Cambridge, 1995)

I Hadn't Meant to Tell You This by Jacqueline Woodson (Bantam Doubleday Dell, 1994)

Isabelle the Itch by Constance C. Greene (Puffin Books, 1992)

Jenna's Big Jump by Faythe Dyrud Thureen (Atheneum, 1993)

Just As Long As We're Together by Judy Blume (Bantam Doubleday Dell, 1991)

The Little House books (series) by Laura Ingalls Wilder (HarperCollins Children's Books, 1997)

Lydia by Marilyn Kaye (Harcourt Brace Children's Books, 1987)

The Moon Bridge by Marcia Savin (Scholastic, 1995)

Number the Stars by Lois Lowry (Houghton Mifflin, 1992)

The Road to Memphis by Mildred D. Taylor (Puffin Books, 1992)

Ronia, the Robber's Daughter by Astrid Lindgren (Puffin Books, 1985)

Sarah, Plain and Tall by Patricia MacLachlan (Harper & Row, 1987)

The Saskiad by Brian Hall (Houghton Mifflin, 1997)

A Separate Peace by John Knowles (Holt, Rinehart and Winston, 1990)

Summer of My German Soldier by Bette Greene (Bantam Doubleday Dell, 1993)

Switching Well by Peni R. Griffin (Puffin Books, 1994)

Tell Me If the Lovers Are Losers by Cynthia Voigt (Atheneum,1982)

To Kill a Mockingbird by Harper Lee (Holt, Rinehart and Winston, 1989)

Treasures from Grandma by Arleta Richardson (Chariot Victor Publishers, 1994)

Turning Thirteen by Susan Beth Pfeffer (Scholastic, 1988)

Under a Different Sky by Deborah Savage (Houghton Mifflin, 1997)

The Voice on the Radio by Caroline B. Cooney (Delacorte Press, 1996)

Walk Two Moons by Sharon Creech (HarperCollins Children's Books, 1996)

Whatever Happened to Janie? by Caroline B. Cooney (Laurel Leaf, 1994)

Where You Belong: A Novel by Mary Ann McGuigan (Simon & Schuster Children's Books, 1997)

Books (nonfiction)

Our favorite books about friendship activities, advice, and some great books on adult friendship, too.

The Best Friends Book by Arlene Erlbach (Free Spirit Publishing, 1995)

The Diary of Latoya Hunter: My First Year in Junior High by Latoya Hunter (Crown Publishers, Inc., 1993)

Games and Giggles Just for Girls by Stacey Schett (Pleasant Company Publications, 1995)

Girlfriends by Carmen Renee Berry and Tamara Traeder (Wildcat Canyon Press, 1995)

Girls Know Best: Advice for Girls from Girls on Just About Everything by Michelle Roehm (ed.) (Beyond Words Publishing Company, 1997)

Great Girl Food: Easy Eats & Tempting Treats for Girls to Make by Jeannette Wall (ed.) (Pleasant Company Publications, 1996)

Helen Keller: The Story of My Life by Helen Keller (Bantam Classics, 1990)

How to Make (and Keep) Friends by Elizabeth Karlsberg (Troll, 1990)

On Women and Friendship by Starr Ockenga (Stewart, Tabori & Chang, 1993)

Respecting Our Differences by Lynn Duvall (Free Spirit Publishing, 1994)

Your Emotions, Yourself: A Guide to Your Changing Emotions by Doreen L. Virtue (Lowell House Juvenile, 1996)

Magazines

NEW MOON

The Magazine for Girls and Their Dreams is the only magazine for girls 8–14 that is edited and written by girls. It lets girls be themselves, connects them with other girls, and listens to them on the issues they really care about.

(800) 381-4743   •   www.newmoon.org

AMERICAN GIRL

(800) 254-1278   •   www.americangirl.com

CICADA

(800) 827-0227   •   www.cricketmag.com

GIRLS' LIFE

(888) 999-3222 • www.girlslife.com

TEEN VOICES

(888) 882-TEEN • www.teenvoices.com

Internet

www.newmoon.org

The inside scoop on *New Moon,* with stories from the magazine, contests, and other fun interactive features.

www.cybergrrl.com

A fun, activity-filled site with comics, interactive adventures, and a chat room.

www.cyberteens.com

A great interactive site, with games, art galleries, and chat rooms.

www.feminist.org

For young teenage girls who are interested in exploring feminist issues, this Feminist Majority homepage is a good first stop.

www.girlpower.com

Featuring personal writing from young teenage girls.

www.girlslife.com

A site by *Girls' Life* magazine, including links to cyberpals, music, and more.

www.gsusa.org

The site introducing you to the Girl Scouts of the U.S.A.

87

www.gURL.com

A site where girls can chat, get advice, play games, and read stories.

www.nwhp.org

The Web site of the National Women's History Project, which seeks to educate the public about the important contributions women have made throughout history.

www.teenvoices.com

An on-line magazine written by and for young women, with articles that challenge traditional gender stereotypes, as well as a chat room.

www.tlounge.com

The TLounge is a Web site by Tampax Tampons for young women, offering points of view, stories, and interviews from all kinds of female writers.

www.troom.com

Enter the TRoom for information on sports, health, music, and travel.

www.unicef.org/voy

The UNICEF "Voices of Youth" site — an educational and fun site where young people from across the globe can interact and learn about the world.

www.women.com

An on-line magazine for women and girls, chock-full of information and interactive forums.

www.yahooligans.com

Yahoo!'s site for kids has everything that *www.yahoo.com* does, but it is aimed right at you.

THE NEW MOON BOOKS GIRLS EDITORIAL BOARD

BACK ROW, LEFT TO RIGHT: Julia Peters-Axtell, Katie Hedberg, Flynn Berry,
Morgan Fykes, Lauren Calhoun, Caitlin Stern, Priscilla Mendoza

FRONT ROW: Elizabeth Larsson, Ashley Cofell

The first convening of the New Moon Books Girls Editorial Board
New York City
May 1998

To read more about the New Moon Books Girls Editorial Board, check
out their bios on the New Moon Web site: www.newmoon.org.

Celebrate and empower girls and women with New Moon Publishing!

"New Moon Publishing has an agenda for girls and young women that's refreshingly different from mainstream corporate media. New Moon is building a community of girls and young women intent on saving their true selves. New Moon's magazines are a godsend for girls and young women, for their parents and the adults who care about them."

—**Mary Pipher, Ph.D.,** author of *Reviving Ophelia: Saving the Selves of Adolescent Girls*

New Moon: The Magazine for Girls and Their Dreams
Edited by girls ages 8–14, *New Moon* is an ad-free international bimonthly magazine that is a joy to read at any age!

New Moon Network: For Adults Who Care About Girls
Share the successes and strategies of a worldwide network of parents, teachers, and other adults committed to raising healthy, confident girls.

Between the Moon and You
A catalog of delightful gifts that celebrate and educate girls and women. Visit at www.newmoooncatalog.com.

New Moon Education Division
A variety of interactive workshops and compelling speakers for conferences or conventions.

For information on any of these New Moon resources, contact:

New Moon Publishing
P.O. Box 3620
Duluth, MN 55803-3620
Toll-free: 800-381-4743 • Fax: 218-728-0314
E-mail: newmoon@newmoon.org
Web site: www.newmoon.org